Love...An Illusion?

Alesha Sherman

Independently Published

Dedication

For My Girls: Briana & Sarai

I hope you will learn from my mistakes. Put God first and He will give you the desires of your heart. Always remember that you can do anything you set your mind to.

Acknowledgments

Abba, I thank you for continued persistence and persuasion in getting me to write this book.

My mom, who when I told her I wanted to write a book she just said, "Okay, do it!" Thanks, mom, for your consistent prayers. I know many of my blessings are because of your prayers.

To my prayer partners who consistently petitioned the throne of God asking Him to give us the strength, to listen to His leading to do His will. This is in answer to our many prayers.

Special thanks to my lifelong sister-friend Simone, who took time out of her busy days to edit and give her opinion and motivation. You have always been a blessing to my life.

To my other friends and family, who I am sure would have supported and encouraged me if I had shared with you my plan to write this book. Surprise!

Contents

Chapter 1: Young and Blind 9

Chapter 2: Do You Only Love Once? 14

Chapter 3: Carrying the Hurt.................................25

Chapter 4: He's Not Mine! 34

Chapter 5: Will I Ever? 39

Chapter 6: The Center of It All 42

A New Perspective 47

About the Author 48

Introduction

Here is a journey into the twisted mind of a confident, beautiful, intelligent, sometimes not so confident, single, and loving it, woman. Sometimes I wish I had someone to hold me. Oh heck! Are you sure you even want to continue reading this book? Well, am I really doing this? I am such a private person, but I am about to share how I truly feel about being single. Well, here goes!

So, how does it feel being single? Well, I enjoy my singleness. I can work on being the best version of me, travel, plan outings with my girlfriends, well the few that I have anyways. I only have to think about what I want and how I feel. Though I enjoy being single, there are days that I would definitely enjoy the company of a partner. There are days I would love for my best friend to be coming on my trips, holding my hand, kissing my forehead, telling me how he loves everything about my body, even my pudge I have been working so hard to lose. There are days when I'm confident that he's out there, and we'll meet when the time is right. Or we have already met and will finally realize we were meant to be together. Then, there are days when it seems that I have just got to accept the fact that I'm going to remain single, that there is no one out there for me, and I was just created to be one of those single women who never get married or never remarry after the death of a spouse, or after a divorce. Am I pretty much destined to be like my mother and her sisters? Oh, do not get me wrong. They chose to remain single after whatever happened, and they all seem to be content. They raised their children well and are now enjoying their grandkids. But I don't think I would make it living that life, but technically I kind of already am.

In all honesty, there are days when I wonder if the fact that I would like a partner means that I'm going to have to settle. Maybe I should just settle instead of being lonely. Hmmmmm, I'm not so sure about that one.

Maybe I'm the only one with all these roller coaster feelings. Some days I'm confident and on a high, then bolted into a flip spin upside down twist of emotions on other days. Hey, I don't even know what each day is going to be. I must say though that my confident days supersedes my crazy emotional days.

Does love even exist or is it just an illusion?

Young and Blind

1

Of course, like every other girl. I dreamed of meeting my prince charming, getting married, having children, and living happily ever after. However, this was such a fairy tale.

So, here I was at seventeen about to turn eighteen, leaving home for the first time to go to college. I met this guy who was about eight years my senior. Of course, you think you are so in love and he is much older, with his own apartment and car and, oh my goodness, yes, he's the one. And of course, being so young and having an older man showing interest, makes you feel good. He was my first!

I was brought up in a Christian home. It was always my goal to follow the biblical principles and to, you know, get married to someone that I am equally yoked with, have children and live happily ever after. However, my life did not follow that pattern. So, here I was at seventeen, pregnant, my last year of community college, doing 'A' level exams, about to transition to a four-year university. Nobody plans on being pregnant at seventeen and to be honest, I never wanted to carry this pregnancy. But, yeah, he was not about to have any of my crazy thoughts. So, I was still thinking okay, even though this has happened, it is not going to be the end of the world. We are going to make it. We are going to have a family. I am going to finish school, and we are going to get married and live happily ever after. Kind of, yeah, no!

I am happy that I had my daughter, but if I could get a 'do over' I would have waited. I would have wanted to do it God's way. It would have eliminated much of the unnecessary drama that came as a result of my poor choices.

My greatest fear was telling my mom. This is surely going to break her heart. So, luckily for me, I have a brother who I can talk to about anything without feeling judged. We planned how to break the news to her. Back then only the very rich had cell phones so I had to drive to the telephone booth to make the call back home. My mom was very upset, of course, because nobody wants that for her child. But despite her being disappointed and upset, her love was still quite evident. My entire family as a matter of fact, was disappointed but supportive. I am grateful for my mom, family members, and friends who were my support system during that time.

Getting pregnant was not easy at that age, in a country where it was very much a taboo to be pregnant early, especially when you are in school. So, I was embarrassed. It was hard dealing with being pregnant and going to school and people having so much to say. I mean, it took an enormous amount of strength and resilience to not worry about what people were saying and just to move forward with what I had to do. When my boyfriend would take me to school, I no longer wanted to be dropped off at the front entrance. There was a back entrance that us students hardly used because there was a very steep hill to climb so we hardly ever took that entrance into the school. Well, being the only girl pregnant on campus and embarrassed, this was the entrance I took. Then I had to speak to administrators, to let them know the situation. Luckily for me, there was nothing in the rulebook that suggests that I had to drop out. This was not high school but college, so I could continue going to classes in preparation for my exams.

Now, I do not remember what the conversation was about or how it ended up happening, but I was separated from my peers. I was put in a class by myself. My teachers would come to that room to teach the lesson. I don't remember how it happened or who made that decision, but I had an Economics teacher, oh my goodness, I can't recall her name, but she was the one who advocated for me to be back with my regular classmates. So I was brought back to the general population. As I look back I can see how your peers can either make you or break you, but for me they were very supportive. If they were saying or thinking anything, it was never done in my presence. I was always accepted and even spoiled sometimes. I want to say a big thank you to my two best buddies during that period of time – Trudy-Ann and Shelly-Ann. I know I made your lives quite difficult but you ladies were troopers, hahaha. There were definitely other students on campus who weren't in my class, who weren't my friends who had a lot to say. They would verbalize it as I was passing by, or whatever, but I had to find that willpower, that motivation, to not allow anything that was said or done in my hearing or otherwise to bother me. And so, in my country, they would say, you develop 'thick skin'.

For my 'A' Level exams, I was sitting four courses, General Studies, Government and Politics, Economics and Sociology. My daughter came at 30 weeks, approximately 4-5 days before my first exam. That was the only course that I received a passing grade for. By then, motherhood had begun which made it impossible for me to have adequate rest and study time for my exams. After completing my exams I made the decision to go back home. I resat my exams and transitioned to University the year after. My mom kept my baby girl and off I went. However, I realized how difficult it was for my mom and despite her protest, after my first year, I made the decision to stay home, work full-time and attend evening classes. With the support of family and friends and the grace of God, I was able to complete my Bachelor of Science in Counselling.

Facing people back home was not easy. People had a lot to say! Sure, they did, because their skeletons were still hidden while mine was on display. But again, you must, at that point, develop the resilience of not letting anything bother you. Put those blinders on, you only need to focus on what is ahead.

Being young and blind and thinking, '*I know what I'm doing*', results in many of us finding ourselves in challenging, life changing situations. Whether it is getting pregnant out of wedlock, making the choice to commit an abortion, taking drugs, or getting raped. Some of us seem to think that it is only people who are from a certain socio economic group, or from a certain community end up in certain situations, but we have to take our blinders off. Some of us were brought up 'the right way". The child of a teacher, pastor, doctor etc. News flash, life does not see social class. Life is life and life happens! No one sets out to make bad decisions or to completely ruin his/her life. None of us have those intentions. Some of us pride ourselves on making good decisions. However, how many of us make perfect decisions all the time? But there comes that time where we make one decision that changes our lives forever. Either we were so blind with infatuation, or we totally ignored the red flags. So here I was at eighteen years old, a single mother of a beautiful baby, who is now a gorgeous, brilliant young lady. What was the journey life then had in store for me?

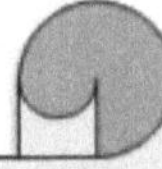

Reminders

Jeremiah 29:11 "For I know the plans and thoughts that I have for you,' says the LORD, 'plans for peace and well-being and not for disaster, to give you a future and a hope." (AMP)

Lynda Randle – God On The Mountain (sing it)

Do You Only Love Once?

2

Ughhhh! Well, I guess I have to tell my real age. So I am about to be 40 years old. I have only truly loved once in my life. Is that okay?, I don't know. But what I do know is, I am grateful for the experience of having loved someone and at some point feeling that love being reciprocated. I have often heard it said that 'you only love once' but who really knows?

In the previous chapter, I told you about how I got pregnant early, but was still able to attend college because of the profound support I had. Now fast forward to after my college years, having completed my Bachelors of Science, unable to then find a job, and not wanting to go into the classroom as a school counselor. I made the decision to work in the private sector. This was my first real job and I met Morris (Mr. Bowlegs) – I loved the shape of his legs…hahaha. I was very interested in getting to know him. However, he was in a relationship so that was the end of that.

Months passed and then our mutual friend indicated that Morris wanted us to exchange numbers. At this point, his previous relationship had ended and so I exchanged numbers. We became really good friends, which I thought was very important as it did set the stage for an amazing relationship. We did not jump straight into a relationship. We took the time getting to know each other, meeting his friends, meeting my friends, meeting family members etc. you know, everything you do when you're in a relationship with someone. We pretty much had a solid relationship as the months and the years evolved. We started talking about and planning for the future. He was an amazing father figure to my little girl. I was in love! . There was a new housing development in our area, so we went to look at the homes, inquire about down payment, all the jazz. However, because this was my first job out of school, we had not accumulated a lot of savings so we weren't able to take advantage of the homeowner's loan. We decided to forego that for the moment but at least we had an idea of what we needed to work towards.

Without a doubt, I saw myself getting married and raising a family with Morris. Had we stayed together, we would now be celebrating over seventeen years together. But, let me tell you, this woman's intuition or whatever you choose to call it, it's real! When you feel like something is not right, it's a high probability that you are correct. However, when these feelings (sixth sense) occur, it is time to pay attention. I'm not into checking phones/emails etc. The minute you get to that stage, it is time to go. So I wasn't checking phones or anything like that. However, sometimes you notice little things and you dismiss it. Well, he always, always, during the course of the relationship, always had his phone near and dear to him. He took it to the bathroom, had it even while cooking in the kitchen. The phone was never left out. It was always on his person.Then, I'd always notice it. But I now realize that I somehow dismissed that 'red flag', because in my head, I'm like, oh, we spend so much time together, we are together almost always.

Eventually we both transitioned into different careers, careers that were within our field of study. He was on a major project and had to live in another city as it was impossible to commute. I visited one weekend and we had a great weekend. It didn't start out so well because I decided to show up unannounced and he had driven to another city. As a result, I had to wait for him to get back and I wasn't happy about that, so I made a big deal (yeah yeah yeah, I know). This was the Friday evening. On Saturday we decided to drive back to our hometown. When we got home, he left to go and visit his family. Okay sure, no problem. However, it was late and he had not returned. I was getting worried. I called and texted his phone, no response. Of course, I went to bed very anxious and upset. This was totally out of character.

Sunday morning and I was still in a frenzy wondering what's going on, what happened? Nothing. So I decided at this point to call his sister in law. So I called his sister in law. She said I have something to tell you. She said, can you meet me now? His sister in law said to me, look he's been living a double life for a long time. I was shocked. It blew me away!

He has someone else; they bought a house together and that is where he is. That is where he has been since he dropped you off on Saturday. She proceeded to tell me that when she was getting married the invitation was given for him plus one. She said, he was asked who he was taking to the wedding. So, basically, the short of it is, he decided to go to the wedding alone, because there were some members of his family that knew her and didn't know me and vice versa, then there were other members of the family that knew of both of us. So, he decided to go by himself. To this day, I really do not remember the explanation he gave me for not taking me to the wedding. And to be honest, thinking back I cannot remember being upset about not being able to go to his brother's wedding. We were together for five years at this point. I had a good relationship with his brother and sister in law. How was it that I was not upset about not going to their wedding? Strange, isn't it?

There must have been other 'red flags' that I dismissed leading up to this. How many times do we see 'red flags' and find justifications for these actions? We need to stop. The minute we see a 'red flag', we need to follow up. We need to start thinking and strategizing and analyzing. Why is it that this is a 'red flag' for me? Get the answers you need, if the answers do not make sense, then act accordingly. Put your next plan into action.

Morris gave everything I wanted to this other woman: His love, his time, the house I wanted, and building a future with him. Then, his sister in law called him on the phone in my presence. Remember, he was not answering my calls or text messages or anything since that Saturday night. However, that Sunday morning, he answered her call right away. His sister in law told him that I was right there, and that she had just told me everything. She then proceeded to call her husband – his brother. He confirmed that his wife was not lying, and that his brother had to be stopped. This had been going on for our entire 'relationship'. Our entire relationship was indeed a fraud!

His sister in law said, " Listen to me, I want you to cry all you want. I want you to scream and cry for the rest of the day. But then, after today, I do not want you to shed one more tear for him. After today, I want you to pick yourself up and I want you to be strong and I want you to carry on with your life, without him." Easier said than done, right? I was dying inside. I just wanted to holler, to scream, to cry. But I did not. I composed myself well, kept it all in. Of course, you know there were tears but not the crying and the hollering that I wanted to do.

It was not surprising that Morris started calling and texting after he was MIA for so long. I wanted him out of the house, I wanted all his things gone! I told him to come and get his stuff or they would be outside on the curb. And to be honest, I think I poured bleach all over them. I never ever wanted to see him or to speak to him again. I was devastated! This deception had been going on for the entire five years of our relationship. I knew of this young lady but I was told she was an ex girlfriend. Technically, I was the other woman.

Morris pledged his undying love for me, and how remorseful he was. He said he truly loved me. He indicated that he met her first. He was her first and he just felt badly about ending things knowing how she felt about him. But then he met me and truly fell in love and I was the person he wanted. What confusion! I was somehow, to believe that.

Looking back, I saw them – the 'red flags': the phone always being in his possession and couldn't be left anywhere, the fact that I knew some of his family members, but not all of them. I questioned not being introduced to them all. I don't remember the answer I was given but obviously, I made sense of the nonsense I was told. I also remember we were taking a taxi home one evening, in my country you become familiar with the taxi drivers as they maintain a specific route. I remember coming home that night, and the taxi stopped at a particular apartment. And he said to the taxi driver that this was not our destination, so the taxi kept driving. The reason I did not find that strange, was because he had a cousin who lived in that apartment building. However, I also remembered that his so-called ex-girlfriend also lived in that apartment building. Well, what he said was that they grew up together in the same community, they were intimate a few times, but they did not have a formal relationship. For me, that was in the past and I had no problem if they were formal with each other. I am never the girl that says, you need to delete her number, unless I am given a reason to make such a request. See, I do believe that there are some people who are capable of maintaining friendships with people whom they've been with in the past, and they're able to keep it professional and cordial and not cross any lines. And so, that was never a red flag for me.

I also remember that she lived in that building, because one morning we were taking my daughter to school. As we were driving by she made a comment. I did not hear clearly what was said but her body language made my alarm bells go off. Again, I was given an explanation which I obviously accepted. So, how many red flags have I counted already?

There came a point where in the back of my head I knew something wasn't right, and I could not shake this feeling, so I began to pray. I asked the Lord, if he is not the person for me, allow something to happen, so that I will know that he is not for me. I am sure some of those red flags were signs that the Lord was giving to me. However, I decided to accept the explanations and to shelve it. But, the Holy Spirit (woman's intuition) continued to bother me. I went back to my God, and I prayed and I asked for another sign, I said, "Lord, if this is not the person for me, or if something is wrong, allow something to happen, something that I cannot overlook". Now, come on. There is no coincidence that I said to the Lord, to allow whatever to happen to be so big that I cannot overlook it. Looking back, that specific phrase tells me that I felt it and that I saw little red flags, and that deep down, I probably realized that little things were coming to light which I was overlooking. So, the only practical thing to do was to present my request to my Abba. I went back on my knees.

This dramatic event that began that Saturday evening was the 'thing' that happened that I could not overlook. Ladies I cannot begin to describe how I felt, knowing that for five years, I gave 110% and the entire five years was a lie. I could not fathom who could do that. And to be honest, despite everything that happened, if Morris had said, Hey, I am truly sorry, I want to make this work. Give me another chance. I mean, even though they bought a house together and all of that, I honestly think if he had taken that step, I would have worked it out and taken him back. But my God did not allow him to do that because He knew that I would have taken him back.

Despite the fact that he gave me the sign that I cannot overlook, I would have taken him back; I would have justified why it was okay to take him back. Probably the justification to myself would be something like:

1. The Lord made it happen, so that everything would come to light, resulting in him ending it with her. And then we would work on our relationship.

2. The Lord probably made it happen, because He knew that there is no perfect relationship. We are going to go to couples counseling and we will make this work.

3. The devil always tries to destroy something good. We would become a power couple with great things ahead, and so the devil wanted to destroy all this.

I am telling you guys; I would have justified taking him back. But my Abba would not allow it. He would not allow it! Did I mention that we were unequally yoked? He would take me to church and pick me up but he had only accompanied me to church once. And I am someone that goes to church every Saturday. I was born in the Seventh Day Adventist Church, and religion, faith etc is a big part of my life.

It is also a big deal for me that whoever I am going to be with should share the same morals, values and belief systems. So, Mr. Bowlegs, and I shared certain morals and values, but not certain beliefs. How would we have raised our children? Whose belief would we have taught our children?

Although I was willing to go against what I believed to be right, God said no. He said, that is not how it works. If I am going to bless your relationship, it cannot go against my words. And his words are plain in 2 Corinthians 6:14 "Do not be unequally bound together with unbelievers [do not make mismatched alliances with them, inconsistent with your faith]. For what partnership can righteousness have with lawlessness? Or what fellowship can light have with darkness?" (AMP)

Unequally yoked does not only refer to religion, but it also refers to other aspects of our lives. It refers to our other belief systems, morals, values, future plans. Everything should align equally across the board. I am not saying that your opinions on everything will be the same, but as it relates to your foundation, morals, values, religious beliefs, rearing of children, future plans, finances - those should align.

So, despite what I wanted, God said you asked me to show you if this was it, this is me showing you that this is not it. So, instead of Mr. Bowlegs coming back to say, I am sorry, let us make it work, he dove straight into other relationships.

For me, the hurt was so much that I didn't want to speak to him or hear from him. I wanted nothing to do with him. Let me not forget to mention that he gave me an explanation. She had told him she was pregnant, hence the reason for him going there that Saturday evening. And he was not going to leave her when she was pregnant. Even though that's not the person he claimed he wanted, he did not want his child to grow up without a dad like he did. That added to my anger because at the end of the day, he was still choosing her over the person he 'loves'. I couldn't understand any of it. He told me that he sought help. He had asked for help from friends and family and they only said that he had to make a decision for himself. I was mad at him for seeking help from others who were living the same lifestyle he was. I made reference to several other mutual friends who were married men, with strong Christian beliefs, men who would have guided him according to biblical principles. That was one of his biggest mistakes.

This was enough, all his explanations were only making me feel worse. At this point I knew that I had to separate myself from him. I could not see or talk to him. I had to keep loving him from a distance because I love me more!

It takes a very strong person to let go of something that he/she truly wants. Yes, there are those days that you still want to hold on. It is like watching cartoons and the devil is on one shoulder and the angel is on the other. It is a battle. But it takes a strong will power to walk away. Whatever you're going through, whatever Morris situation you are in, believe me, you have the strength, you can do it. You can let go, deep down you know you need to get out of this situation. You deserve better!

Pray, fight this battle on your knees. There is a God, and He will give you the strength you need. Confide in friends, or family members who will hold you accountable, who will pray with and encourage you, who will be your support system through that time. Do not send or reply to that text, instead call your prayer circle to help you withstand the urge. It is not easy, trust me, I know.

But, once you do it, it becomes easier and easier. Then throughout your life, it becomes so much easier to walk away from situations you do not belong in.

I was torn to pieces, heartbroken, devastated. This was my first love. Would this be my last? I never gave up on meeting someone else or falling in love again. It just never happened. Did I want to? Absolutely! But the hurt was too much to allow me to open myself to love or be loved by someone else. Oh, how I was hurting!

Reminders

2 Corinthians 6:14 "Do not be unequally bound together with unbelievers [do not make mismatched alliances with them, inconsistent with your faith]. For what partnership can righteousness have with lawlessness? Or what fellowship can light have with darkness?" (AMP)

Romans 8:28 "And we know [with great confidence] that God [who is deeply concerned about us] causes all things to work together [as a plan] for good for those who love God, to those who are called according to His plan and purpose." (AMP)

Lynda Randle - He Will Carry You (sing it!)

Carrying the Hurt

3

So here I was heartbroken, wondering, how did this happen? I saw my entire life with this guy. Now, one thing that I did not do was to deal with the hurt. Instead, I lived with the hurt. Big mistake!

This resulted in two things happening:
1. I ended up hurting others. We all know that common saying – 'hurting people, hurt people'.
2. I ended up making the biggest mistake of my entire life.

So, let me tell you about the first mistake, me hurting others. So here I was hurting from a five-year relationship that I thought was going to move into marriage, children, and the whole works. Of course, I had friends, co-workers, neighbors who were always interested in being more than friends. However, they always respected the fact that I was in a committed relationship, so it never went beyond just being friends. So, I decided the best way to get over Morris was to hangout as much as possible with friends and have fun. I started hanging out with a friend. We were friends for years at this point, went to the same church, involved in common community service activities, and shared mutual friends. You get the point. I chose someone I had no interest in and I thought he had no interest in me.

However, later on in talking to one of my best friends (more like a sister) she actually told me she realized that he was always into me but she never did say anything to me. Well I started hanging out more with Anthony (Mr. Not My Type), I was still hurting so I only wanted to be distracted from the pain. My first mistake was that we were hanging out by ourselves when our other friends were unavailable. First rule broken - if you are going to be hanging out with any guy, it is best to always be in a group of friends.

Well we started kissing and things rapidly progressed from there. I started seeing a lot more of Anthony (Mr. Not My Type). We were going to the movies by ourselves and hanging out with his sister at his house. The one thing I did make clear to him was that if Morris got his 'ish' together it was a wrap. I had no apologies for saying it and I meant every word of it. He knew my relationship had ended but to this day he has no idea why. So, he knew right away that I was not about to cross certain lines, because this was not what I wanted.

We continued this for months. People started assuming we were a couple, but of course, we both kept denying it. This was someone who was never my type in terms of looks or personality – he was the very quiet, shy type. However, the more time I spent with him, I realized he was

such a gentleman, who is very family oriented. We shared the same religious beliefs but unequally yoked at that time in terms of future plans, finances etc. I, on the other hand, was moving forward with things that I wanted to accomplish, things I had planned with Morris.

I was open to dating other people because I knew Anthony and I were not heading in the same direction. And so, I met the biggest mistake of my life. It was at that time that Anthony decided to communicate his true feelings for me. But at that point it was too late because I had met David (Mr. Biggest Mistake Ever) and I was moving in that direction.

I ended up pregnant. It seemed as if Anthony (Mr. Not My Type) was willing to forgive me and progress into the next level of our relationship, even though I was pregnant with someone else's child. He never did communicate this, but I inferred this from his actions towards me. People thought he was the father of my unborn child, but we both knew that was impossible. Anthony waited until it was too late to share exactly how he felt. I cannot blame him for that, because remember, I made it abundantly clear that this was going nowhere, and that the minute Morris (Mr. Bowlegs) blinked his eyes at me, I was running back into his arms. I ended up hurting someone who absolutely did not deserve to be treated the way I treated him. For that I am truly sorry. He is an awesome person who I am sure will make someone very happy.

I was now ready to start the next chapter of my life with someone I thought would make a good partner. It was the biggest mistake of my life and I saw many, many, many 'red flags'. He was a great pretender but eventually his true colors started showing. We started living together, preparing for the birth of our child. It was at this time I started seeing him for who he truly was. He was my worst nightmare. I mentally planned my exit strategy before giving birth to our child. I already knew I was not sticking around for this. Living with this person was toxic. When he goes to work, I would use his computer, only to find him communicating with other women via Skype (that was the thing back then), certain mails were left in his driver's car door and some taken into the house. I would find receipts for flowers or dinner in his pants. No flowers were coming home to me! I cooked so that there was food at the house when he got home from work. On the days that I was not cooking, he was away. He chose to leave me at home to go and have dinner whether by himself or with someone, I don't know. At that point, I did not care because I already knew I was leaving after giving birth.

My worst nightmare would be very passive-aggressive, emotionally abusive. He would accuse me of all the things that he was doing. To be honest, I do not doubt that I was also passive-aggressive, because at that point, I was totally unhappy. I was ready to go. I never argued with him about the receipts or messages I found, so keeping all that in probably did make me passive-aggressive.

I eventually informed him I was leaving about two months before my due date. I told him I did not want my (our) child to grow up seeing him treating me this way, thinking this is how a man is supposed to treat her. He was never physically abusive, but there was no guarantee it would not have gotten to that point. There was always a high probability that verbal abuse can transition into physical abuse. I absolutely refused to live that life. I had never encountered that in my entire life up to that point and I was not about to live that life. Nope, nope, nope.

I wanted to leave North Carolina for Florida, but of course he refused to take me. I said, okay, that's fine. I will book a ticket. I have never been totally reliant on any one person and I never will be. Ensure that you are making your own money or as a homemaker, put aside a little out of every bit given to you to take care of the house. If you do not have your own money, is there a friend or family member that you can call on? Do not be afraid to confide in someone about what is happening. They may be the one to help you get out, to buy you a plane, bus or train ticket out.

As for him refusing to take me, I made him aware that I was leaving with or without his help. So, I said, 'Are you driving me or should I book my ticket?' I was leaving and he was mad. Less than a month after having my baby, I was out of there. David (Mr. Biggest Mistake) continued to be toxic to my well-being. It has continued to be a toxic co-parenting situation. The level of toxicity destroyed me mentally and physically.

Take time to heal! When we don't, we find ourselves in situations that we would have never ended up in. Had we been in the right frame of mind we would not have made certain decisions; we would not have said certain things or acted a certain way. Healing is not a quick process. It is ongoing, we have to work at it daily. You work on yourself, reminding yourself of who you are, where you see yourself going, what your plans and goals are. And you start working on those.

It is very easy to start another relationship, very easy, but what are you bringing to this other relationship? Are you bringing with you the hurt from the previous relationship that you have not dealt with? Are you bringing the broken pieces of yourself? Now, this other person has no idea that you have a lot of baggage, this other person has no idea how to help, because you do not even know how to help yourself. They cannot make you whole. You must work on making yourself whole. Seek professional help. This allows you to be given the strategies needed to overcome your hurt.

What I did was to bring pieces of a jigsaw puzzle. I brought some pieces to Anthony (Mr. Not My Type), then other pieces to David (Mr. Biggest Mistake). So, my pieces were all over the place. They both had some, and I had some, and I probably left some with Morris (Mr. Bowlegs). How can we put this puzzle together, to make the beautiful portrait it should be? It will never happen because the pieces are all over the place. So, we have to take time to heal. Take time to put that puzzle back together. It is broken, it is torn, some of the pieces are lost. Take the time to look for the lost pieces.

Find someone you can talk to, a friend or professional, someone who will be brutally honest. Since high school, my friends and I have always said, if we cannot be 100% honest with each other then we should not be friends. A true friend should be able to tell you where you went wrong with love, not be judgmental. They should be able to give recommendations on how to work towards fixing the issue. And you should be able to accept the positive criticisms. I have some of the best friends ever, one in particular who I can trust, to be completely honest. Simone is going to be brutally honest, yes it might hurt hearing, hmmm, well not might; It WILL hurt hearing the truth, but it is all coming from a place of love. And because I know this, I am confident telling her anything.

Feel the pain, acknowledge it but do not get stuck. Work through it. Cry if you need to cry, talk, scream, journal. Do whatever works for you. I journal my pain in prayers to Abba. CrossFit has not only become a lifestyle change, but a way of channeling my stress or hurt.

After the hurt and the healing, several years later, that is, I was able to remain friends with Morris (Mr. Bowlegs). One reason is because he was like one of best friends before transitioning into us being a couple. He also had a lot of issues that he needed to work on too. So he had to heal too. It was just recently that there was a dynamic change to our friendship. To this day, I cannot tell you what it is. But it's okay. At this point in my life, I am not concerned. I do believe that people come into your life for a reason, or a season and if his season in my life is over, I am at peace with that. So I have never asked, nor will I ever try to find out why we don't communicate as we use to, anymore. As for Anthony (Mr. Not My Type) after we had both healed; we were able to discuss what had happened and apologized for the part we played. We have continued being friends.

However, there are some people, that in order to heal, you have to completely separate yourself from them because they are so toxic. And that is perfectly fine! As for David (Mr. Biggest Mistake), he will forever be a part of my life. However, I have had to learn how to deal with it, I had to separate myself from him in so many ways, because the toxicity was permeating every aspect of my life. I was giving him the power to continuously ruin my mental state which affected every other aspect of my life. Every day I would pray asking God to help me to forgive him and to more importantly, forgive myself. See, my friend Dean- who only came into my life for season, helped me to see that my hatred for David was destroying me and blocking the many blessings the Lord wanted to bestow on me. I was badgering myself about how stupid I was getting involved with this person and how I deserved the lifelong repercussions. But, my Abba helped me to see that how I was treated was ALL about who he is as a person, and had nothing to do with me.

Sidenote – he did the exact same thing to someone else.

I implemented strategies of how to communicate with this person for the rest of my life. Yes, set whatever boundaries you need to for *your* wellbeing. We will only communicate on topics concerning our child. Once I have said what I need to, there will be no tit for tat, no more response from me to any of his messages. He is blocked from my social media and WhatsApp, no verbal calls, or text messages. Emails only. This allows me to respond to only what is necessary. Of course, he has unlimited access to his child, and I try my best to shield her from any drama, hence the reason for the strategies I have implemented.

Be mindful of the decision you make. It will either positively or negatively impact you or those around you. And I cannot stress enough, take time to heal. When you are healed and whole and you are then able to put all the pieces of your jigsaw puzzle together, you are now ready to share your whole, beautiful, intelligent self with someone. My healing came through a lot of prayer and fasting and pleading with the Lord to take the pain away. There is a God who can carry/take your burdens so you can be free from the weight of whatever is pulling you under.

Reminders

Romans 5: 3-5 "And not only this, but [with joy] let us exult in our sufferings and rejoice in our hardships, knowing that hardship (distress, pressure, trouble) produces patient endurance; and endurance, proven character (spiritual maturity); and proven character, hope and confident assurance [of eternal salvation]." (AMP)

1 Peter 5:7 " casting all your cares [all your anxieties, all your worries, and all your concerns, once and for all] on Him, for He cares about you [with deepest affection, and watches over you very carefully]."(AMP)

Isaiah 40:29 "He gives power to the faint and weary, and to him who has no might He increases strength [causing it to multiply and making it to abound]." (AMP)

Kirk Franklin – He'll Take the Pain Away" (sing it)

He's Not Mine!

4

How many of us venture into relationships where the other person is emotionally unavailable? Weeeell, I have! he/she is either someone else's husband/wife, boyfriend/girlfriend or just not ready for a committed relationship. Whatever the case, he/she is just not yours.

Many of us pretend we do not know what the outcome is going to be, but be real, it is obvious. You cannot change people into being ready for a committed relationship just because you treat them well or give them 150% of yourself when they are only giving 50%. It will not change them into being ready, but they will continue enjoying all the perks you allow. Access to your bedroom or any touching you allow, means you are playing the role of a wife: meal preparation, laundry, living together etc.

For a lot of us, especially women, who are more emotional, feelings change rather quickly, especially when physical intimacy comes into play. Therefore, while you started out as friends with benefits, eventually you start wanting more. No matter how we tell ourselves that we can detach, it does not always play out that way. This is why the Bible speaks about sex before marriage, because emotions take over once sex comes into the picture. However, if you refrain from sexual intimacy, then you are truly getting to know the person without your emotions clouding your judgment or overshadowing the red flags that you may see.

So here I was with someone who was emotionally unavailable. Now, he laid all his cards on the table, did not hide anything, was totally upfront about everything, However, of course he was willing to participate in any extracurricular activity I was willing to allow. I weighed the pros and cons of the situation. To be honest, the outcome was obvious in my head, but for whatever reason, I decided to still go ahead with this person who was emotionally available.

I did not expect any changes on his side. However, eventually, I wanted to see him more, something he was not able to offer based on his personal circumstances. I was thinking of this person more often than I should. Then the mental battle began. Is he even thinking of me? Does he miss me? Here I was setting myself up because nothing good could come of this situation. It was a battle between having fun with this person and feeling guilty about what I was doing. What was wrong with me? How stupid can I be setting up myself to be hurt again and how could I do this to another woman? I had experienced the pain of a failed relationship – a cheating partner. Am I really doing this to someone else?

Making the decision to be with someone that is emotionally unavailable is just basically going to take you through a rollercoaster of emotions. This will result in deep seated emotional battles and you will never be prepared to handle the outcome, later on, trust me! Come on, did you really think he/she was going to leave his/her spouse or significant other? Remember, the fact that you knew he/she was emotionally unavailable that was basically your answer that nothing will change. We sometimes consciously set ourselves up. We sabotage our own happiness. Whatever short term 'happiness' or fulfillment you are getting out of these relationships are miniscule compared to the emotional battles that it will bring and the emotional scars that are going to resurface.

I felt as though every time I took twenty steps forward; I then took fifty steps back. And for many of us, we start questioning whether we will truly find a life partner or why the Lord has not answered our prayers. Some of us at this point decide to settle. This happens because we are also emotionally unavailable. Unavailable because we are still working through past hurt, unforgiveness, self-love etc. Did you take the time to just work on you?

Many of us think that we must be in a relationship. It is okay to be single. Being single is fun. You can travel, spend your money the way you want to, have no one to answer to about your whereabouts or finances…hahaha! If you are a single mom, you need a break. Leave your child(ren) with trustworthy family members or friends. Take time to regroup and have fun, do something you have always wanted to.

I just simply cannot continue to make bad choices, to give myself to men who do not deserve me, people who are not worth my time. How can I expect God to answer my prayers when I am here doing everything wrong? I have to constantly remind myself that God cannot go against His Word. He is eager to fulfill His promises to us. So, you have been praying for years or months for the Lord to come through for you in some way. I can confidently say He is working on it. We may not be able to see it, but He *must* fulfill His promise. However, you can be sabotaging the work the Lord is doing. How are you waiting? How you wait is important. If you are waiting while having an extramarital affair with your neighbor, you are blocking the work that the Lord is doing. If you are waiting while sleeping with random people, then you are sabotaging the work the Lord is doing.

Your prayers are being heard by the Lord. He is working on answering our prayers. He is preparing your husband/wife for you. But when we are focused on these emotionally unavailable men/women, we do not see the person that we are praying for on the other side. He has been trying to get our attention, but we are distracted. And so, it is not that God is not answering our prayers, it is just that we are sabotaging the work that He is doing. We have to position ourselves to receive what we are asking of Him.

Be honest, how do you really feel after being with this person? Yes, the Lord made us sexual beings, it feels good, but after, are you riddled with guilt? When you are at home feeling sad or depressed about something or just feeling blah, are you able to call this person to really talk about how you are feeling? Is this person there for you? Is it worth the emotional roller coaster? Don't you deserve more? WHAT ARE YOU WORTH?

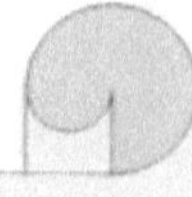

Reminders

1 Corinthians 13: 4-5 "Love is patient, love is kind. It does not envy, it does not boast, it is not proud. It does not dishonor others; it is not self-seeking…" (AMP)

1 Corinthians 6:20 "You were bought with a price [you were actually purchased with the precious blood of Jesus and made His own]. So then, honor and glorify God with your body." (AMP)

Donald Lawrence – **Deliver Me** (sing it)

Will I Ever?

5

Will I ever! I cry as I write these words. I will, because I am going to claim every promise in his book, his words cannot return unto Him void. I do not know about you, but I believe in a mighty God. I believe there is some celestial being in Heaven that is looking down on all of us, and dying for us to claim the promises He has given us:

1. John 14:14 "You may **ask** me for **anything** in my name, and I will do it." (NIV)
2. Mark 11:24 "For this reason I am telling you, whatever things you ask for in prayer [in accordance with God's will], believe [with confident trust] that you have received them, and they will be given to you."
3. Jeremiah 29:11-12 " For I know the plans I have for you," declares the Lord, "plans to prosper you and not to harm you, plans to give you hope and a future. Then you will call on me and come and pray to me, and I will listen to you."

Did I mention the one in

4.   Isaiah 60:22 "At the right time, I, **the LORD, will make it happen.**"

So, if you should ask me that question again. Will it ever happen for me? Yes, it will happen for me. The only person that can block what the Lord has in store for me, is me. You are the only person that can block what God has in store for you. There are so many times when God is steering us down a certain path and every time we start along the path, we detour, telling ourselves 'I am strong enough to stop and turn around when I am ready.' We make the conscious decision to choose the opposite of what the Lord wants.

Romans 7: 15-20 "For I do not understand my own actions [I am baffled and bewildered by them]. I do not practice what I want *to do*, but I am doing the very thing I hate [and yielding to my human nature, my worldliness—my sinful capacity]. Now if I *habitually* do what I do not want to do, [that means] I agree with the Law, *confessing* that it is good (morally excellent). So now [if that is the case, then] it is no longer I who do it [the disobedient thing which I despise], but the sin [nature] which lives in me. For I know that nothing good lives in me, that is, in my flesh [my human nature, my worldliness—my sinful capacity]. For the willingness [to do good] is present in me, but the doing of good is not. For the good that I want to do, I do not do, but I practice the very evil that I do not want. But if I am doing the very thing I do not want to do, I am no longer the one doing it [that is, it is not me that acts], but the sin [nature] which lives in me. It is a constant battle between good and evil.

God cannot go contrary to his word. And so if He says that He will give us the desires of our hearts, He WILL give us the desire of our hearts, but we cannot be on Satan's side, I am ready to stop doing me and do God. Will it ever happen for me? Yes.

Jeremiah 32: 27, he says, "I am the Lord, the God of all mankind is anything too hard for me?" He can help us to stop being interested in someone that is emotionally unavailable, someone that we are unequally yoked with. I have a very vivid imagination. Some of the things I can envision would blow your mind. If we submit ourselves to Him, He is able to do abundantly more than we could even ask or imagine in our lives (Ephesians 3:20). Then will it ever happen? Yes, it will happen.

Paul, In speaking to the Corinthians, told us that it is better to marry than to burn. (1 Corinthians 7:9) God does not want us to sit there watching porn, fornicating, committing adultery. So, if that means that He needs to give us a husband or a wife, He will. He is a man of his word, we can completely trust in Him. There is no heartache with this guy. Demand His promises, claim them. Be the best version of yourself. He is ready and willing to work with us to achieve that.

Reminders

Numbers 29:11 "God is not human, that he should lie, not a human being, that he should change his mind. Does he speak and then not act? Does he promise and not fulfill?" (NIV)

Emmanuel Quartet – Jesus Never Fails (sing it)

The Center of It All

6

So many of us are hurting from failed relationships, or no relationships. But we need to realize that a lot of what we are enduring now, the pain, discomfort, if we are honest with ourselves, was because of us not ordering our steps in the Lord's way. Also, as a result of us not following our intuition (our mind). This is generally the Holy Spirit, directing/ guiding us. And so a lot of the times we say, you know, if I had followed my mind this would not have happened, my mind was telling me not to do this or not to go this far. We sensed it, we heard it, but we chose to do what we wanted to. And a lot of us make that conscious decision to live in that feel-good moment, to settle for momentary orgasms. In whatever way these orgasms come, remember they are fleeting.

Despite our setbacks, all we need to do is to refocus, center ourselves. And there is only one person at the center of it all. And that is our Abba! His promises are true, He cannot go back on His word, and He reminds us that He will never leave us, nor will He ever forsake us. As parents, do we forsake our children when they are disobedient to our instructions? Do we love them any less? No, we do not! Instead, the repercussions for their actions may be to punish them or have a discussion. Either way, we do this out of love to instill/teach the importance of obedience, the importance of right from wrong, and how to make good choices.

So, why do we tend to forget that Abba, our dad, loves us even more than our earthly parents? So, yes, there will be repercussions for our actions because He loves us. I am prepared to put on my big girl panties and handle those consequences. In the midst of handling those consequences, we run directly to Him, clinging to Him, asking for His help. Unlike man, He does not have a hands-off approach, He is right there pulling us through, helping us through the consequences of our actions. He loves us, despite our shortcomings.

Recenter yourself!

Heartaches are a part of the process for those of us that consistently choose our own way. We settle for emotionally unavailable individuals, unequally yoked partners. We live mediocre lives not living up to our fullest potential etc., that feel-good moment of just being able to say, I have a boyfriend/girlfriend, being able to post pictures on social media, the temporary feeling of having someone lying beside you. Through all this, is Abba the *Center of It All?*

We are robbing ourselves of the happiness, contentment that God wants to give us. And I know a lot of you are probably going to say it is easier said than done. That is a fact! It is so sad that there are so many of our friends who are married, parents or other singles who are so judgmental. Some will say just pray about it, you will be okay, Hahaha. I have to laugh, prayer definitely works and is our source of strength, absolutely. But let me make reference again to the Apostle Paul's statement in Romans 7: 15 "For I do not understand my own actions [I am baffled and bewildered by them]. I do not practice what I want to do, but I am doing the very thing I hate [and yielding to my human nature, my worldliness—my sinful capacity]"

King David was an adulterer and murderer (Read his story in 2 Samuel 11&12)

Apostle Paul was a murderer (read his story in Acts 9)

Peter – failed many times (read his story in Matthew 14-16)

Rahab – prostituted herself (read her story in Joshua 2)

Samson – women were his weakness -unequally yoked (read his story in Judges 13-16)

These men and women were used by God. He never turned his back on them. He was nonjudgmental. Certain things are not the easiest for everyone, and the fact is, some of us need to stop being so judgmental of each other. We need to be that source of support to say, I know exactly what you are going through, I was there. Let us see how we can work together to get you where you want to be. (Girls/Guys night out, fasting & prayer). When we are real with each other, and share our experiences, it helps us, strengthens us, because it prevents some of us from feeling like failures.

Remember we have the Lord already answering our prayers before we come to Him, the Holy Spirit is also petitioning Him to help us before we even ask. Look at that, someone has got our backs, multiple people at that, because He knows 'the struggle is real.'

Stop looking at other friends, social media. Yeah, yeah, yeah they are posting pictures with their boo, going out on dates, taking trips. Yes, we all want that, but what are we willing to sacrifice? Give social media a break, even some friends, if it is making it harder to deal with your situation. And just so you know, you would be surprised to see the difference between social media and real life. Recenter yourself with Him, The Center of it All!

Like Lot's wife, let us not get stuck in that moment because we are afraid to let go of what the Lord is asking us to leave behind. Let go. Move forward. Even if your arms are stretching behind you, trying to hold on to it, do not look back, keep moving. Do not get stuck in that position as Lot's wife did.

We take many risks daily. When we get in our car to drive, that is a risk because we do not know if we are going to make it back home. We do not even know if we are going to make it to our destination and we do this without a second thought. Why then, are we not willing to take the 'risk', in letting God be the center of it all?

I will find someone that chooses to love me and I, him. Together we will practice unconditional love that comes only through putting the other person first. We will make many sacrifices and forgiveness. It will be hard work. I am ready to open my heart to find that love, and it all comes with following God's direction.

I am ready to let go of the things I know I should, to earnestly take time to talk to God daily, to allow him to show me the things and people I need to separate from. Are you ready to do the work? Whether it is spending more time in his presence, working on yourself, taking time to heal, seeking professional help. Just ensure that when you are looking to speak to someone, you find someone that believes in God, and has God as the center of his/her life.

Is anything too hard for our God? Absolutely not. He is the

Center of it all. So, this illusion of love can become my reality. I am trusting him. Will you?

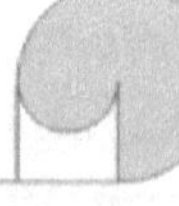

Reminders

Ephesians 3:20 – "Now to Him who is able to [carry out His purpose and] do superabundantly more than all that we dare ask or think [infinitely beyond our greatest prayers, hopes, or dreams], according to His power that is at work within us." (AMP)

Job 42:2 - "I know that you can do all things; no purpose of yours can be thwarted." (ESV)

Deitrick Haddon – He's Able (sing it)

Jonathan McReynolds – God is Good (sing it)

Jonathan McReynolds – Lovn' Me (sing it)

Israel Houghton & New Breed – Jesus At the Center (sing it)

A New Perspective

The Lord is disappointed when His people place a low estimate upon themselves. He desires His chosen heritage to value themselves according to the price He has placed upon them. God wanted them; else He would not have sent His Son on such an expensive errand to redeem them. He has a use for them, and He is well pleased when they make the very highest demands upon Him, that they may glorify His name. They may expect large things if they have faith in His promises.

Desire of Ages, page 668

About the Author

Jamaican woman by birth and is the epitome of a strong woman who is, 'little but tallawah.'

She is a God fearing, proud mother of two beautiful girls. She loves cats, enjoys reading a good book and the company of great friends.

Alesha holds a Bachelor of Science in Counselling and is a fun loving person who will become a forever friend once you get to know her.